Edward O. Lord

The American Poultry and Pigeon Fanciers' and Breeders'

'Directory

Edward O. Lord

The American Poultry and Pigeon Fanciers' and Breeders' 'Directory

ISBN/EAN: 9783337144746

Printed in Europe, USA, Canada, Australia, Japan

Cover: Foto ©Andreas Hilbeck / pixelio.de

More available books at **www.hansebooks.com**

THE AMERICAN

POULTRY AND PIGEON

FANCIERS' AND BREEDERS'

DIRECTORY,

SHOWING THE VARIETY FANCIED AND BRED BY EACH PERSON.

Copyrighted and Edited by EDWARD O. LORD.

PRICE, FIFTY CENTS PER COPY.

GREAT FALLS, N. H.:
PUBLISHED BY E. O. LORD & CO.
1881.

THE AMERICAN

POULTRY AND PIGEON

FANCIERS' AND BREEDERS'

DIRECTORY,

SHOWING THE VARIETY FANCIED AND BRED BY
EACH PERSON.

Copyrighted and Edited by EDWARD O. LORD.

——— ———

PRICE, FIFTY CENTS PER COPY.

——— ———

GREAT FALLS, N. H.:
PUBLISHED BY E. O. LORD & CO.
1881.

U. S. DIRECTORY.

PART I.

Gallinaceous Division.

CLASS I.—ASIATIC.—LIGHT BRAHMAS.

CONNECTICUT.

C. K. Bond	Oakville
Fred W. Goodale	Danbury

MAINE.

Mrs. R. W. Sargent	Kittery

MASSACHUSETTS.

R. G. Buffinton	Somerset
Eldridge C. Comey	Somerville
Thomas G. Colt	Pittsfield
Philander Williams	Taunton

MARYLAND.

T. A. Rommel	Baltimore

MICHIGAN.

O. R. Shaw	Kalamazoo
John T. Strong	Lansing

NEW HAMPSHIRE.

C. B. Dubois	Nashua
Dubois & Thompson	Goffstown

NEW JERSEY.

C. S. Cooper   Schraalenburgh
P. A. Conners   Orange, Essex Co
Westervelt Haywood   Rutherford

NEW YORK.

William B. Burnett   Johnstown
J. Wilson Jones   Utica, N. Y
Frank D. Lewis & Bro   Amsterdam
F. F. Preston   Candor
Chas. E. Rockenstyne   Albany
S. K. Wilcox   Smyrna, Chenango Co

PENNSYLVANIA.

T. Fletcher   West Monterey
. Herman   Erie
J. A. Roberts   Malvern, Chester Co
P. F. & John Spakr   Carlisle

CLASS I.—ASIATIC.—MISCELLANEOUS.

NEW YORK.

C. T. Fletcher   Jamestown

CLASS I.—ASIATIC.—DARK BRAHMAS.

OHIO.

F. A. Matthis   Bryan

PENNSYLVANIA.

Potts Bros   Parkesburg
P. F. & John Spakr   Carlisle

RHODE ISLAND.

H. J. Reynolds   Providence

CLASS I.—ASIATIC.—BUFF COCHINS.

CONNECTICUT.

C. K. Bond   Oakville

MISSOURI.

A. Kurtz   Platte City

MASSACHUSETTS

Edward W. Staples   Taunton

NEW JERSEY.

John Van Mater   Colt's Neck

NEW YORK.

James Haynes   Stockport, Col. Co
H. B. Minor   Sagerties

PENNSYLVANIA.

P. F. & John Spakr   Carlisle

CLASS I.—ASIATIC.—PARTRIDGE COCHINS.

CONNECTICUT.

Fred W. Goodale   Danbury
C. M. Gilman   Southport

ILLINOIS.

Geo. V. Frink   Bloomington, McLear Co

MASSACHUSETTS.

Daniel P. Shove   Somerset
H. A. Jones   Worcester

NEW YORK.

Chas. E. Rockenstyne   Albany

NEW JERSEY.

John Van Mater   Colt's Neck

OHIO.

F. A. Matthis   Bryan

PENNSYLVANIA.

L. E. Burgess   Providence, Lacka Co
O. Hemstriel   Wilkesbarre
P. F. & John Spakr   Carlisle

Starr L. Booth   Bristol

CLASS I.—ASIATIC.—WHITE COCHINS.

KENTUCKY.

J. L. Shallcross   Louisville

MASSACHUSETTS.

R. G. Buffinton   Somerset
Edward W. Staples   Taunton

NEW YORK.

E. J. Eichenberg   Waverly

CLASS I.—ASIATIC.—BLACK COCHINS.

CONNECTICUT.

C. K. Bond   Oakville
W. W. Walker   Bridgeport

MASSACHUSETTS.

R. G. Buffinton   Somerset
Geo. W. Lovell   Middleboro
A. E. Smith   Cherry Valley
Edward W. Staples   Taunton
E. Frank Webster   Haverhill

NEW JERSEY.

Jas. K. Little   Belleville

NEW HAMPSHIRE.

Prentiss & Litchfield   Keene

PENNSYLVANIA.

E. N. Denman   Greensburg
P. F. & John Spakr   Carlisle

CLASS I.—ASIATIC.—BRAHMAS.

CONNECTICUT.

W. W. Walker   Bridgeport

7

MASSACHUSETTS.

N. K. Felch   Natick
Philander Williams   Taunton

NEW JERSEY.

Wm. H. Remsen   Whitehouse Station

NEW YORK.

Foyles Bros   Greenbush, Rens Co
James Haynes   Stockport, Col. Co
J. R. Sheldon   Hornellsville
T. C. Van Wyck   Poughkeepsie

OHIO.

W. H. Todd   Vermillion

PENNSYLVANIA.

T. M. Nelson   Chambersburg
S. S. Yarnall   Phoenixville

CLASS I.—ASIATIC.—COCHINS.

MAINE.

Mrs. R. W. Sargent   Kittery

MASSACHUSETTS.

Philander Williams   Taunton

NEW YORK.

T. C. Van Wyck   Poughkeepsie

OHIO.

W. B. Evans   Ripley

PENNSYLVANIA.

T. M. Nelson   Chambersburg

CLASS II.—GAME.—BLACK-BREASTED RED.

ILLINOIS.

C. A. Keeper   Sterling

8

MASSACHUSETTS.

Geo. R. Purrinton	Somerset
Edward W. Staples	Taunton

NEW YORK.

Kicarstead & Smith	Clear Creek
Chas. E. Rockenstyne	Albany
S. K. Wilcox	Smyrna, Chenango Co
Carl Waite	Springville

OHIO.

H. M. Brooks	Andover

PENNSYLVANIA.

E. N. Denman	Greensburg
A. P. Fox	Ashley
J. T. Fletcher	West Monterey
Homer H. Hewitt	Williamsburg
J. R. Lichty	Lancaster
P. F. & John Spakr	Carlisle

CLASS II.—GAME.—WHITE GAME.

CONNECTICUT.

J. Schofield	Seymour

CLASS II.—GAME.—S. DUCKWING.

PENNSYLVANIA.

J. R. Lichty	Lancaster

CLASS II.—GAME.—W. GEORGIAN.

PENNSYLVANIA.

P. F. & John Spakr	Carlisle

CLASS II.—GAME.—MISCELLANEOUS.

NEW YORK.

John H. Derby	Sandy Hill
H. Kellogg	Brainard Sta
E. H. Phelps	Morris

9

OHIO.

W. H. Todd   Vermillion

PENNSYLVANIA.

J. T. Fletcher   West Monterey

CLASS III.—GAME BANTAMS.—BLACK-BREASTED RED.

MASSACHUSETTS.

Daniel P. Shove   Somerset

NEW YORK.

W. C. Card   Morris
S. K. Wilcox   Smyrna, Chenango Co

PENNSYLVANIA.

A. P. Fox   Ashley

CLASS III.—GAME BANTAMS.—YELLOW DUCKWING

CONNECTICUT.

Fred W. Goodale   Danbury

NEW YORK.

F. W. Gaylor   Nassau

CLASS III.—GAME BANTAMS.—S. DUCKWING.

CONNECTICUT.

Fred W. Goodale   Danbury

MASSACHUSETTS.

R. G. Buffinton   Somerset

NEW YORK.

T. C. Van Wyck   Poughkeepsie

OHIO.

W. B. Evans   Ripley

10

CLASS III.—GAME BANTAMS.—RED PILE.

CONNECTICUT.

R. G. Wilson — Bridgeport

NEW YORK.

F. W. Gaylor — Nassau

CLASS III.—GAME BANTAMS.—MISCELLANEOUS.

MASSACHUSETTS.

R. G. Buffinton — Somerset

NEW YORK.

G. F. Allison — Clark's Mills
John H. Derby — Sandy Hill
Foyle Bros — Greenbush, Rens Co
F. W. Gaylor — Nassau
Ranson B. Jones — Penn Yau

PENNSYLVANIA.

F. Herman — Erie

CLASS IV.—HAMBURGS.—GOLDEN SPANGLED.

VERMONT.

C. C. Paine — East Bethel

CLASS IV.—HAMBURGS.—SILVER SPANGLED.

MASSACHUSETTS.

H. A. Jones — Worcester

NEW YORK.

Daniel Hubbs — Jonesville
Kierstead & Smith — Clear Creek

PENNSYLVANIA.

P. F. & John Spakr — Carlisle

VERMONT.

C. C. Paine — East Bethel

CLASS IV.—HAMBURGS.—BLACK.

NEW YORK.

Chas. Bennington   Pittsfield, Otsego Co
Chas. E. Rockenstyne   Albany

PENNSYLVANIA.

J. T. Fletcher   West Monetery
J. M. Long   London, Franklin Co
Potts Bros   Parkesburg

VERMONT.

C. C. Paine   .   East Bethel

CLASS IV.—HAMBURGS.—SILVER PENCILED.

PENNSYLVANIA.

P. F. & John Spakr   Carlisle

CLASS IV.—HAMBURGS.—MISCELLANEOUS.

NEW YORK.

C. F. Fletcher   Jamestown
Foyle Bros   Greenbush, Rens Co
C. A. Paterson   Gate, Watervliet

OHIO.

W. H. Todd   Vermillion

CLASS V.—SPANISH.—WHITE LEGHORNS.

CONNECTICUT.

Dr. J. W. King   Kent

KENTUCKY.

J. L. Shallcross   Louisville

MASSACHUSETTS.

R. G. Buffinton   Somerset

MISSOURI.

A. Kurtz   Platte City

NEW YORK.

F. S. Gardner	Smyrna
S. D. Howland	Schuylerville
Charles E. Rockenstyne	Albany
S. K. Wilcox	Smyrna, Chenango Co

PENNSYLVANIA

J. T. Fletcher	West Monterey
A. J. Pontims	Millersburg

CLASS V.—SPANISH—BROWN LEGHORNS.

ILLINOIS.

C. A. Keefer	Sterling

MAINE.

Mrs. R. W. Sargent	Kittery

MASSACHUSETTS.

Frank A. Dorr	Chestnut Hill
Edward W. Staples	Taunton

MICHIGAN.

George Humphrey	Pontiac

NEW JERSEY.

R. Vanderhoven	Rahway

NEW YORK.

George H. Burgott	Lawton Station
A. F. Conger	Lawton Station
S. D. Howland	Schuylerville
Charles E. Rockenstyne	Albany
Jerry Sharpe	West Sand Hill, Rens Co

PENNSYLVANIA.

C. W. Canfield	Athens, Bradford Co
J. T. Fletcher	West Monterey
J. M. Long	London, Franklin Co
George D. Lewis	Clifton Heights
Potts Bros	Parkesburg

VERMONT.

′ Thorn & Tasker   Brattleboro

CLASS V.—SPANISH.—DOMIQUE LEGHORNS.

MASSACHUSETTS.

A. L. Leach   Newbury

NEW YORK.

F. W. Shafard   Camdem, Oneida Co

VERMONT.

C. C. Paine   East Bethel

CLASS V.—SPANISH.—BLACK SPANISH.

MICHIGAN.

George Humphrey   Pontiac

NEW YORK.

O. Beebe   Hamilton

PENNSYLVANIA.

George D. Lewis   Clifton Heights

CONNECTICUT.

George A- Cosgrove   Whitneyville

VERMONT.

C. C. Paine   East Bethel

CLASS V.—SPANISH.—ROSE COMB WHITE LEGHORNS.

CONNECTICUT.

N. D. Forbes   New Haven

NEW YORK.

C. F. Barbar   Ithaca
F. W. Cowles   Canandaigus
L. B. Drake   Ovid
L. A. Foote   Deansville, Oneida Co

14

PENNSYLVANIA.

George D. Lewis   Clifton Heights

VERMONT.

C. C. Paine   East Bethel

CLASS V.—SPANISH.—ROSE COMB BROWN LEGHORNS.

MASSACHUSETTS.

D. M. Spooner   Lawrence

NEW YORK.

L. A. Foote   Deansville, Onedia Co
Kiearstead & Smith   Clear Creek

NEW HAMPSHIRE.

C. B. Dubois   Nashua

C. C. Paine   East Bethel

CLASS V.—SPANISH.—LEGHORNS.

MASSACHUSETTS.

James L. Bowen   Springfield
Thomas G. Colt   Pittsfield
C. F. Sargent   Lawrence

NEW JERSEY.

H. F. Alling   Newark
S. R. Nevius   North Branch

NEW YORK.

Dr. Jas. A. Draper   Troy
C. F. Fletcher   Jamestown
F. B. Zimmer   Gloversville

OHIO.

W. H. Todd   Vermillion

PENNSYLVANIA.

W. K. Crities	Huntingdon
Homer H. Hewitt	Williamsburg
Dr. G. J. Mead	Erie

PENNSYLVANIA.

George W. C. Stein & Son	Philadelphia

CLASS V.—SPANISH.—W. F. B.

PENNSYLVANIA.

P. F. & John Spakr	Carlisle

CLASS VI.—DORKINGS.—SILVER GRAY.

MASSACHUSETTS.

C. A. Strong	Plymouht

PENNSYLVANIA.

George D. Lewis	Clifton Heights

CLASS VI.—DORKINGS.—COLORED.

MASSACHUSETTS.

H. A. Jones	Worcester

NEW YORK.

S. K. Wilcox	Smyrna, Chenango Co

CLASS VI.—DORKINGS.—MISCELLANEOUS.

MAINE.

Mrs. R. W. Sargent	Kittery

MASSACHUSETTS.

James L. Bowen	Springfield

NEW JERSEY.

C. O. Poole	Metuchen

CLASS VII.—POLISH.-WHITE CRESTED BLACK.

NEW YORK.

Amos G. Day	Ithaca
S. B. Howland	Schuylerville
Chas. E. Rockenstyne	Albany

NEW JERSEY.

R. Vanderhoven	Rahway

PENNSYLVANIA.

P. F. & John Spakr	Carlisle

VERMONT.

C. C. Paine	East Bethel

CLASS VII.—POLISH.—H. C. W.

NEW YORK.

Chas. E. Rockenstyne	Albany

CLASS VII.—POLISH.—BEARDED WHITE.

PENNSYLVANIA.

P. F. & John Spakr	Carlisle

CLASS VII.—POLISH.—BEARDED GOLDEN.

PENNSYLVANIA.

P. F. & John Spakr	Carlisle

CLASS VII.—POLISH.—GOLDEN.

MASSACHUSETTS.

James Davis'	Fall River

CLASS VII.—POLISH.—WHITE.

NEW YORK.

Amos G. Day	Ithaca

CLASS VII.—POLISH.—BUFF.

MASSACHUSETTS.

James Davis   Fall River

CLASS VII.—POLISH.—SILVER BEARDED.

NEW YORK.

Chas. E. Rockenstyne   Albany

CLASS VII.—POLISH.—MISCELLANEOUS.

NEW YORK.

Rev. C. W. Bolton	New Rochelle, Westchster Co
Foyles Bros	Greenbush, Rens Co
T. C. Van Wyck	Poughkeepsie

CLASS VIII.—FRENCH.—HOUDANS.

ILLINOIS.

James E. White   Englewood, Cook Co

MAINE.

Mrs. R. W. Sargent   Kittery

MASSACHUSETTS.

R. G. Buffinton	Somerset
C. F. Sargent	Lawrence
Fred & C. B. Sampson	Springfield

NEW YORK.

H. S. Anderson	Union Springs
Edgewood Farm	Albany
Jno. W. McHarg	Albany
Charles E. Rockenstyne	Albany

OHIO.

W. B. Evans	Ripley
W. H. Todd	Vermillion

18

PENNSYLVANIA.

| J. M. Long | London, Franklin Co |
| P. F. & John Spakr | Carlisle |

CLASS IX.—BANTAMS.—GOLDEN SEBRIGHTS.

CONNECTICUT.

C. K. Bond   Oakville

MASSACHUSETTS.

R. G. Buffinton	Somerset
Edward W. Staples	Taunton
Philander Williams	Taunton

NEW JERSEY.

S. D. Dyer   Voneland

OHIO.

W. B. Hinsdale   Wadsworth

CLASS IX.—BANTAMS.—SILVER SEBRIGHTS.

CONNECTICUT.

C. K. Bond   Oakville

MASSACHUSETTS.

R. G. Buffinton   Somerset

MAINE.

R. S. Melcher   Portland

MICHIGAN.

L. Whittaker   North Adams

NEW HAMPSHIRE.

C. B. Dubois   Nashua

NEW YORK.

| Frank D. Lewis & Bro | Amsterdam |
| Herbert Maycumber | Truxton |

PENNSYLVANIA.

Joseph S. Butler   New Castle

VERMONT.

C. C. Paine   East Bethel

CLASS IX.—BANTAMS.—ROSE COMBED BLACK.

MASSACHUSETTS.

R. G. Buffinton   Somerset

VERMONT.

C. C. Paine   East Bethel

CLASS IX.—BANTAMS.—ROSE COMBED WHITE.

MASSACHUSETTS.

R. G. Buffinton   Somerset

CLASS IX.—BANTAMS.—JAPANESE.

CONNECTICUT.

H. S. Chapman   Saybrook

MASSACHUSETTS.

R. G. Buffinton   Somerset

NEW HAMPSHIRE.

C. B. Dubois   Nashua

CLASS IX.—BANTAMS.—MISCELLANEOUS.

CONNECTICUT.

R. G. Wilson   Bridgeport

MAINE.

Mrs. R. W. Sargent   Kittery

MASSACHUSETTS.

James L. Bowen   Springfield
Philander Williams   Taunton

NEW JERSEY.

J. E. Diehl   Beverley
Westervelt Haywood   Rutherford

NEW YORK.

C. F. Fletcher   Jamestown
J. Kleason   Rochester
H. Kellogg   Brainard Station
F. B. Zimmer   Gloversville

OHIO.

W. H. Todd   Vermillion

PENNSYLVANIA.

Homer H. Hewitt   Williamsburg
W. R. Teeter   Pittston
C. S. Yarnall   Phoenixville

CLASS X.—MISCELLANEOUS.—AMERICAN DOMINIQUES.

NEW YORK.

F. S. Gardner   Smyrna
Gibbs Bros   Westfield
Daniel Hubbs   Jonesville
G. H. Towle   Truxton

CLASS X—MISCELLANEOUS.—SULTANS.

CONNECTICUT.

C. K. Bond   Oakville

CLASS X.—MISCELLANEOUS.—ANDALUSIANS.

MAINE.

Mrs. R. W. Sargent   Kittery

MASSACHUSETTS.

Edward W. Staples   Taunton

NEW HAMPSHIRE.

C. B. Dubois   Nashua

CLASS X. MISCELLANEOUS.—PLYMOUTH ROCKS.

CONNECTICUT.

E. .C Sherwood	Southport
W. W. Walker	Bridgeport

ILLINOIS.

C. A. Keefer	Sterling
James E. White	Englewood, Cook Co

INDIANA.

W. M. Hinchman	Bushville

KENTUCKY.

J. L. Shallcross	Louisville

MASSACHUSETTS.

R. G. Buffinton	Somerset
James L. Bowen	Springfield
Frank A. Dorr	Chestnut Hill
J. K. Felch	Natick
Chas. A. Knapp	Raynham
C. F. Sargent	Lawrence
D. M. Spooner	Lawrence
Fred & C. B. Sampson	Springfield
E. Frank Webster	Haverhill

MAINE.

James H. Banks	Freeport
Dr. G. M. Twitchell	Fairfield

MICHIGAN.

George Humphrey	Pontiac

MISSOURI.

A. Kurtz	Platte City

NEW JERSEY.

C. S. Cooper	Schraalenburgh
A. Leida	Delaware Station
S. P. Nevius	North Branch
R. Vanderhoven	Rahway

NEW HAMPSHIRE.

Dubois & Thompson	Goffstown
C. B. Dubois	Nashua
Prentiss & Litchfield	Keene

NEW YORK.

E. S. Brown	Greenport, L I
C. E. Bush	Hastings, Oswego Co
George Burgott	Lawton Station
F. W. Cowles	Canandaigua
E. Corning	Albany
L. B. Drake	Ovid
C. F. Fletcher	Jamestown
H. C. Leonard	Lowville, Lewis Co
C. A. Paterson	Gate, Watervliet
Charles E. Rockenstyne	Albany
Jerry Sharpe	West Sand Hill, Rens. Co
G. H. Towle	Truxton
Chas. Van Buren	Castleton

OHIO.

F. A. Matthis	Byran

PENNSYLVANIA.

D. S. Feidt	Millersburg
J. T. Fletcher	West Monterey
F. Herman	Erie
Homer H. Hewit	Williamsburg
J. M. Long	London, Franklin Co
George D Lewis	Clifton Heights
T. M. Nelson	Chambersburg
Potts Bros	Parkesburg
Joseph S. Butler	New Castle
P. F. & John Spakr	Carlisle

VERMONT.

Thorn & Tasker	Brattleboro

CLASS X.—MISCELLANEOUS.—LANGSHANS.

CONNECTICUT.

W. W. Walker	Bridgeport

DISTRICT OF COLUMBIA.

Dr. R. H. Evans	Washington

MAINE.

Mrs. R. W. Sargent	Kittery

MASSACHUSETTS.

Chas. H. Marland — Ballardvale

NEW JERSEY.

R. Vanderhoven — Rahway

NEW YORK.

Chas. Bennington — Pittsfield, Otsego Co
C. A. Crum — Pine Grove, Schuyler Co
L. B. Drake — Ovid
C. F. Fletcher — Jamestown
Kierstead & Smith — Clear Creek
Frank D. Lewis & Bro — Amsterdam
H. B. Minor — Saugerties
Charles E. Rockenstyne — Albany
T. C. Van Wyck — Poughkeepsie

PENNSYLVANIA.

L. E. Burgess — Providence, Lacka Co
J. T. Fletcher — West Monterey
M. Hayden & Son — New Milford
George D. Lewis — Clifton Heights

CLASS X.—MISCELLANEOUS.—AMERICAN SEBRIGHTS.

MASSACHUSETTS.

H. C. Seymour — Waltham

NEW YORK.

Gibbs Bros — Westfield
Herbert Maycumber — Truxton
G. H. Towle — Truxton

PENNSYLVANIA.

C. J. Sadler — Pittville, Philadelphia

RHODE ISLAND.

Reynolds & Wakefield — Providence

CLASS X.—MISCELLANEOUS.—BLACK JAVAS.

CONNECTICUT.

J. Schofield	Seymore
H. S. Chapman	Saybrook

MASSACHUSETTS.

R. G. Buffinton	Somerset

NEW YORK.

J. Y. Bicknell	Buffalo
N. T. Lattin	Gaines, Orleans Co

VERMONT.

C. C. Paine	East Bethel

CLASS XI.—TURKEYS.—BRONZE.

MICHIGAN.

L. Whittaker	North Adams

NEW YORK.

O. Beebe	Hamilton
Jerry Sharpe	West Sand Lake, Rens Co

PENNSYLVANIA.

J. T. Fletcher	West Monterey
Homer H. Hewitt	Williamsburg
T. M. Nelson	Chambersburg
Potts Bros	Parkesburg

CLASS XI.—TURKEYS.—MISCELLANEOUS.

OHIO.

W. H Todd	Vermillion

CLASS XII.—ORNAMENTAL SILVER PHEAS-
ANTS.

NEW YORK.

B· F. Beardsley	Binghamton

AQUATIC DIVISION.

PART II.

CLASS XIII.—DUCKS.—WHITE MUSCOVY.

MASSACHUSETTS.

R. G. Buffinton   Somerset

CLASS XIII.—DUCKS.—PEKIN.

CONNECTICUT.

Fred W. Goodale   Danbury

NEW JERSEY.

R. Vanderhoven   Rahway

NEW YORK.

H. B. Minor   Saugerties
Jerry Sharpe   West Sand Lake, Rens Co
S. K. Wilcox   Smyrna, Chenango Co

PENNSYLVANIA.

Potts Bros   Parkesburg

CLASS XIII.—DUCKS.—ROUEN.

NEW YORK.

S. K. Wilcox   Smyrna, Chenango Co

CLASS XIV.—GEESE.—MISCELLANEOUS.

OHIO.

W. H. Todd   Vermillion

CLASS XV.—ORNAMENTAL.—WOOD DUCKS.

MASSACHUSETTS.

R. G. Buffinton   Somerset

MICHIGAN.

Luis A. Leland   Colon, St. Joseph Co

OHIO.

W. B. Hinsdale   Wadsworth

COLUMBARIAN DIVISION.

PART III.—PIGEONS.

CLASS XVI.—POUTERS.—MISCELLANEOUS.

DISTRICT OF COLUMBIA.

E. E. Schreiner	Washington
S. W. Stinemetz	Washington

MICHIGAN.

L. H. Cranston	Marshall

NEW YORK.

N. M. Bingham	Rome
Henry C. Cook	New York City
J. Wilson Jones	Utcia
F. B. Zimmer & Co	Gloversville

OHIO.

W. B. Hinsdale	Wadsworth
L. Simonton	Lebanon
Frank Tallmadge	Columbus
C. H. W. Weber	Cincinnati

CLASS XVI.—CARRIERS.—MISCELLANEOUS.

CONNECTICUT.

R. G. Wilson	Bridgeport

NEW JERSEY.

R. Vanderhoven	Rahway

NEW YORK.

Amos G. Day	Ithaca
J. Kleason	Rochester

OHIO.

W. B. Hinsdale	Wadsworth
C. H. W. Weber	Cincinnati

CLASS XVI.—FANTAILS.—SMOOTH-HEADED.

MASSACHUSETTS.

John G. Howland	Worcester
Jesse M. Rutler	Lawrence

OHIO.

Frank Tallmadge	Columbus

VERMONT.

C. C. Paine	East Bethel

CLASS XVI.—FANTAILS.—CRESTED.

MASSACHUSETTS.

C. A. Ballow	White Calcutta,	Worcester
Chas. L. Chase	" "	Fall River
John G. Howland		Worcester
E. H. Moore		Melrose
Jesse M. Butler	Red Fans,	Lawrence
Edward W. Staples	White Calcutta,	Taunton
Edward W. Staples	Red Fans,	Taunton
Edward W. Staples	Yellow Fans,	Taunton
Edward W. Staples	Black Fans,	Taunton

OHIO.

Frank Tallmadge	Columbus

CLASS XVI.—FANTAILS.—MISCELLANEOUS.

CONNECTICUT.

R. G. Wilson	Bridgeport

DISTRICT OF COLUMBIA.

E. E. Schreiner   Washington
S. W. Stimemetz   Washington

KENTUCKY.

Samuel Casseday Jr   Louisville
L. Shallcross   Louisville

MASSACHUSETTS.

J. G. Howland   Worcester
E. H. Moore   Melrose
D. M. Spooner   Lawrence
Edward W. Staples   Taunton
George Woolley   Waltham

MARYLAND.

F. A. Rommell   Baltimore

MICHIGAN.

L H. Cranston   Marshall

NEW YORK.

N. M. Bingham   Rome
J. Kleason   Rochester
F. B. Zimmer & Co   Gloversville

NEW JERSEY.

R. Vanderhoven   Rahway

OHIO.

C. H. W. Weber   Cincinnati

VERMONT.

Julius J. Estey   Brattleboro
C. C. Paine   East Bethel

CLASS XVI.–ENGLISH OWLS.-MISCELLANEOUS

NEW JERSEY.

Oscar Seifert   Newark

CLASS XVI.—OWLS.

E. E. Schreiner — Washington

MASSACHUSETTS.

H. A. Jones — Worcester
Jesse M. Rutler — Lawrence
George Woolley — Waltham

MARYLAND.

F. A. Rommel — Baltimore

NEW YORK.

N. M. Bingham — Rome

OHIO.

W. B. Hinsdale — Wadsworth
C. H. W. Weber — Cincinnati

PENNSYLVANIA.

Geo. W. C. Stein — Philadelphia

CLASS XVI,—TURBITS.—MISCELLANEOUS.

CONNECTICUT.

R. G. Wilson — Bridgeport

DISTRICT OF COLUMBIA.

E. E. Schreiner — Washington

KENTUCKY.

J. L. Shallcross — Louisville

MASSACHUSETTS.

H. A. Jones — Worcester
E. H. Moore — Melrose
D. M. Spooner — Lawrence
George Woolley — Waltham

MARYLAND.

T. S. Gaddess — Baltimore

NEW HAMPSHIRE.
Edward O. Lord   Great Falls

NEW YORK.
N. M. Bingham   Rome

OHIO.
C. H. W. Weber   Cincinnati

PENNSYLVANIA.
John W. Caughey   Alleghany

CLASS XVI.—TRUMPTERS.—MISCELLANEOUS.

CONNECTICUT.
R. G. Wilson   Bridgeport

DISTRICT OF COLUMBIA.
E. E. Schreiner   Washington

MARYLAND.
T. S. Gaddess   Baltimore
F. A. Rommel   Baltimore

MASSACHUSETTS.
E. H. Moore   Melrose
Philander Williams   Taunton

NEW YORK.
N. M. Bingham   Rome

NEW JERSEY.
Oscar Seifert   Newark

OHIO.
C. H. W. Weber   Cincinnati

CLASS XVI.—TULBLERS.—MISCELLANEOUS.

KENTUCKY.
Samuel Casseday Jr   Louisville

32

MARYLAND.
T. S. Gaddess   Baltimore
MASSACHUSETTS.

Chas. L. Chase   Fall River
C. E Cromach   Stoneham
Herbert Lyman   Waltham

MICHIGAN.
L. H. Cranston   Marshall

NEW JERSEY.
R. Vanderhoven   Rahway

NEW YORK.
N. M. Bingham   Rome

OHIO.
W. B. Hinsdale   Wadsworth
C. H. W. Weber   Cincinnati

PENNSYLVANIA.
John W. Caughey   Alleghany

CLASS XVI.—HELMETS.—MISCELLANEOUS.

MASSACHUSETTS.
E. H. Moore   Melrose

CLASS XVI.—BARBS.—MISCELLANEOUS.

CONNECTICUT.
R. G. Wilson   Bridgeport

MASSACHUSETTS
E. H. Moore   Melrose
George Woolley   Waltham

NEW YORK.
D. E. Newell   New York City
F. B. Zimmer & Co   Gloversville

PENNSYLVANIA.
Geo. W. C. Stein & Son   Philadelphia

33

CLASS XVI.—JACOBINS.—RED

MASSACHUSETTS.

Jesse M. Rutler   Lawrence

CLASS XI.—JACOBINS.—MISCELLANEOUS.

CONNECTICUT.

R. G. Wilson   Bridgeport

DISTRICT OF COLUMBIA.

E. E. Schreiner   Washington

MASSACHUSETTS.

F. L. Allen   Worcester
D. Frank Ellis   No. Cambridge
Herbert Lyman   Waltham
D. M. Spooner   Lawrence
George Woolley   Waltham

MICHIGAN.

L. H. Cranston   Marshall

NEW JERSEY.

R. Vanderhoven   Rahway

NEW HAMPSHIRE.

Edward O. Lord   Great Falls

NEW YORK.

N. M. Bingham   Rome
C. A. Hofheins   Buffalo
J. Wilson Jones   Utica
J. Kleason   Rochester
George E. Peer   Rochester

OHIO.

Frank Tallmadge   Columbus
C. H. W. Weber   Cincinnati

PENNSYLVANIA.

Geo. W. C. Stein & Son   Philadelphia

Julius J. Estey   Brattleboro

CLASS XVI.—MAGPIES.—MISCELLANEOUS.

DISTRICT OF COLUMBIA.

E. E. Schriener   Washington

MASSACHUSETTS.

C. E. Cromach   Stoneham
E. H. Moore   Melrose

OHIO.

Frank Tallmadge   Columbus

CLASS XVI.—RUNTS.—SWALLOWS.

DISTRICT OF COLUMBIA.

E. E. Schreiner   Washington

KENTUCKY.

J. L. Shallcross   Louisville

MASSACHUSETTS.

E. H. Moore   Melrose

MARYLAND.

F. A. Rommel   Baltimore

NEW JERSEY.

Oscar Seifert   Newark.

OHIO.

C. H. W. Weber   Cincinnati

CLASS XVI.—RUNTS.—NUNS.

CONNECTICUT.

R. G. Wilson   Bridgeport

MASSACHUSETTS.

E. H. Moore   Melrose

NEW JERSEY.

Oscar Seifert   Newark

CLASS XVI.—RUNTS.—PRIESTS.

CONNECTICUT.

R. G. Wilson   Bridgeport

MASSACHUSETTS.

E. H. Moore   Melrose

NEW JERSEY.

Oscar Seifert   Newark

CLASS XVI.—RUNTS.—ARCHANGLES.

MASSACHUSETTS.

E. H. Moore   Melrose

NEW HAMPSHIRE.

Edward O. Lord   Great Falls

CLASS XVI.—RUNTS.—ANTWERPS.

MARYLAND.

H. F. Whitman   Baltimore

NEW JERSEY.

R. Vanderhoven   Rahway

NEW YORK.

N. M. Bingham   Rome
Amos G. Day   Ithaca

OHIO.

W. B. Hinsdale   Wadsworth
C. H. W. Weber   Cincinnati

VERMONT.

C. C. Paine   East Bethel

CLASS XVI.—HOMING PIGEONS.

CONNECTICUT.

Geo. Lee   Wauregan

MASSACHUSETTS.

C. E. Cromach   Stomeham
R. T. Paine   Waltham
E. S. Raymond   Fall River

MARYLAND.

H. F. Whitman   Baltimore

NEW JERSEY.

J. C. Decker   Newark
Wm. Verrinder Jr   Jersey City Heights
I. B. Welsh   Jersey City Heights

NEW YORK.

B· F. Beardsley   Binghamton
E. J. Bramhall   Brooklyn
Jos. R. Husson   New York City
J. W. Moore   New York City
Thos. H. Richardson   Green Island
Henry Rover   Brooklyn
Stephen Van Moers   Brooklyn
John Van Opstal   New York City ·

OHIO.

J. C. Decumbe   Cleveland
Frank Tallmadge   Columbus

PENNSYLVANIA.

J. A. Allen   Rochester
D. S. Newhall   Philadelphia

VERMONT.

C. C. Paine   East Bethel

CANADA DIRECTORY.

—

PART II.

Gallinaceous Division.

CLASS I.—ASIATIC.—LIGHT BRAHMAS.

CANADA.

F. J. Grenny	Brantford, Ont
G. H. Pugsley	Brantford, P. O. Ont

CLASS I.—ASIATIC.—DARK BRAHMAS.

CANADA.

G. H. Pugsley	Brantford, P. O. Ont

CLASS I.—ASIATIC.—PARTRIDGE COCHINS.

CANADA.

G. H. Pugsley	Brantford, P. O. Ont

CLASS II.—GAME.—BLACK BREASTED RED.

CANADA.

Chas. M. Nellis	Brantford, P. O. Ont

CLASS III.—GAME BANTAMS.—SILVER DUCKWING.

CANADA.

Chas. M. Nellis	Brantford, P. O. Ont

38

CLASS IV.—HAMBURGS.—BLACK.

CANADA.

G. H. Pugsley   Brantford, P. O. Ont

CLASS V.—SPANISH.—WHITE LEGHORNS.

CANADA.

W. Stahlschmidt   Preston, Ont

CLASS V.—SPANISH.—BROWN LEGHORNS.

CANADA.

W. Stahlschmidt   Preston, Ont

CLASS V.—SPANISH.—BLACK SPANISH.

CANADA.

J. M. Corson   Orangeville, Ont

CLASS V.—SPANISH.—ROSE COMB BROWN LEGHORNS.

CANADA.

C. A. Graft   Fisherville
G. H. Pugsley   Brantford, Ont

CLASS IX.—BANTAMS.—MISCELLANEOUS.

CANADA.

G. H. Pugsley   Brantford, Ont

CLASS X.—MISCELLANEOUS.—PLYMOUTH ROCKS.

CANADA.

F. J. Grenny   Brantford, Ont
G. H. Pugsley   Brantford, Ont

CLASS X.—MISCELLANEOUS.—ANDALUSIANS.

CANADA.

G. H. Pugsley   Brantford, Ont

CLASS X.—MISCELLANEOUS.—LANGSHANS.

CANADA.

C. A. Graft   Fisherville
F. J. Grenny   Brantford, Ont
G. H. Pugsley   Brantford, Ont

CLASS X.—MISCELLANEOUS.—AMERICAN SEBRIGHTS.

C. A. Graft   Fisherville

CLASS X.—MISCELLANEOUS.—BLACK JAVAS.

CANADA.

G. II. Pugsley   Brantford, P. O. Ont

PURE PIT GAMES.

KENTUCKY.

Samuel Casseday Jr   Louisville

NEW YORK.

Harry Lambert   Hinsdale, Col Co
C. S. Salisbury   Naples, Ontario Co

PENNSYLVANIA.

James Coad   Bruin, P. Q.

AQUATIC DIVISION.

CLASS XIII.—DUCKS.—PEKIN.

CANADA.

F. J. Grenny   Brantford, Ont

CLASS XIII.—DUCKS.—ROUEN.

CANADA.

F. J. Grenny   Brantford, Ont

CLASS XV.—ORNAMENTAL.—MADARIN DUCKS.

CANADA.

G. H. Pugsley   Brantford, P. O. Ont

E. J. BRAMHALL,

289 President St., Brooklyn, N. Y.,

Breeder and Fancier

——— OF ———

Homing Pigeons !

☞ Pedigree, Price &c., a matter of correspondence. ☜

ADDRESS,

E. J. BRAMHALL,

289 President Street,   BROOKLYN, N. Y.

EDWARD O. LORD,

GREAT FALLS, NEW HAMPSHIRE.

—IN MY LOFTS ARE—

MANY IMPORTED BIRDS AND PRIZE WINNERS!

——THERE ARE——

Eight Varieties of Jacobins,
Thirty-Seven Varieties of Turbits,
Twenty Varieties of Fantails.

☞ No Birds are shipped C. O. D., but if purchases do not tally in every point with description sent, the Birds can be returned, and their price, less express charges, will be refunded.

Send Stamp for Price List.

Practical Information on Breeding Cheerfully Given to Amateur Patrons.

All letters with stamp enclosed answered.

Express Paid to Boston on All Birds Going South and West.

www.ingramcontent.com/pod-product-compliance
Lightning Source LLC
Chambersburg PA
CBHW031803090426
42739CB00008B/1141